ALPHABETICAL CONTENTS

All My Life

Words by
Joel Hailey

Music by
Joel Hailey and Rory Bennett

Original key: D♭ major. This edition has been transposed down one half-step to be more playable.

I will nev - er find an - oth - er lov - er sweet - er than

you, sweet - er than you. ____ And I will nev - er find an - oth - er

lov - er more pre-cious than you, _____ more pre-cious than you. _____ Girl, you are

close to me, you're like my moth-er, close to me, you're like my fath-er, close to me, you're like my sis-ter,

close to me, you're like my broth-er. You are the on - ly one. _____ You're my ev -

- 'ry-thing and for you _____ this song _____ I sing. _____ all my life _____
And

7

feel the same __ way too. _____ Yes, I

To Coda ⊕

pray that __ you do love __ me too. _____ I said you're

all _____ that I'm think - ing of. _____

Da, da, da, da, da. Da, da, da, da, da. Da, da, da, da, da. Da, da,

9

When you smile life is glow. You picked me up when I was down. And I

hope that ___ you feel the same ___ way too. _____

Yes, I pray that ___ you do love ___ me

too. _____ In all my life ___

12

Because You Loved Me

from UP CLOSE AND PERSONAL

Words and Music by
Diane Warren

Recorded a half step lower.

light in the dark, _ shin-ing your love _ in - to my _ life. ____ You've

been my in - spi - ra - tion. ____ Through the lies ____ you were _ the truth. My

world is a bet - ter place be - cause _ of you. ____ You were _ my

CODA   loved _ me.   You were _ my   strength when I ____ was weak.   You were _ my

Better Be Good to Me

Words and Music by
Mike Chapman, Nicky Chinn
and Holly Knight

that's how it's got to be ___ now,
that's how it's got to be ___ now,

'cause I ___ don't have no use for what ___ you loose-ly call the truth. ___
'cause I ___ don't have the time for ___ your o-ver load-ed lines. ___

___ Oh, you bet-ter be good ___ to me.
___ Oh, you bet-ter be good ___ to me.

Yes, you bet-ter be good. ___
Yes, you bet-ter be good. ___

Butterfly Kisses

Words and Music by
Bob Carlisle and Randy Thomas

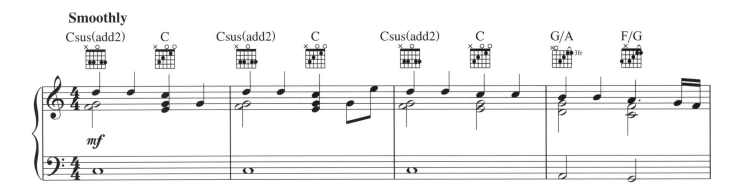

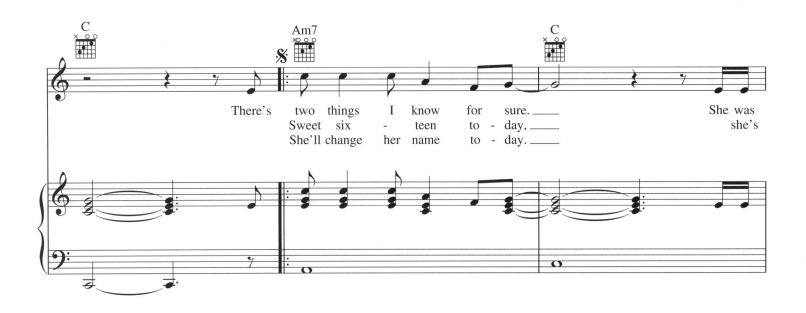

There's two things I know for sure.____ She was
Sweet six - teen to - day,____ she's
She'll change her name to - day. ____

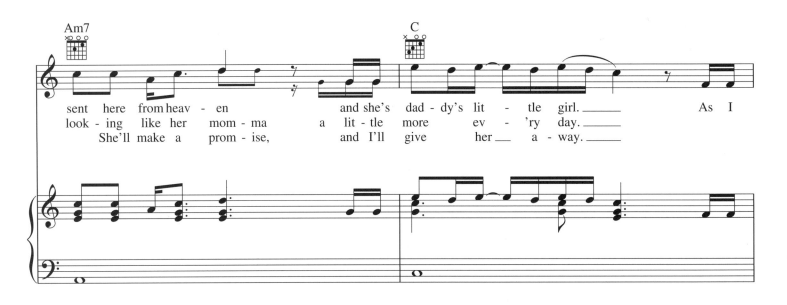

sent here from heav - en and she's dad - dy's lit - tle girl.____ As I
look - ing like her mom - ma a lit - tle more ev - 'ry day. ____
She'll make a prom - ise, and I'll give her ___ a - way. ____

drop to my knees ___ by her bed _____ at night, ___
One part wom - an, the oth - er part girl. To
Stand - ing in the bride room just star - ing at her,

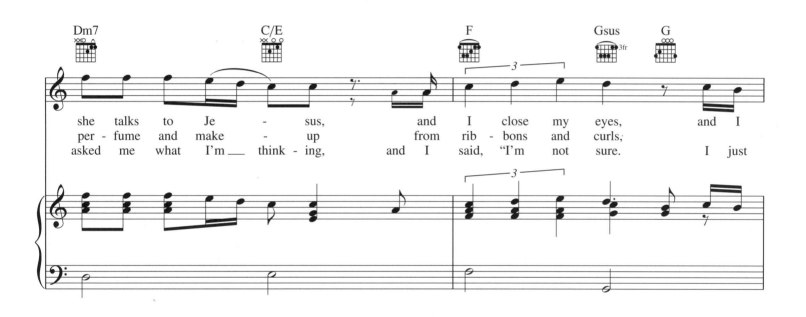

she talks to Je - sus, and I close my eyes, and I
per - fume and make - up from rib - bons and, curls;
asked me what I'm ___ think - ing, and I said, "I'm not sure. I just

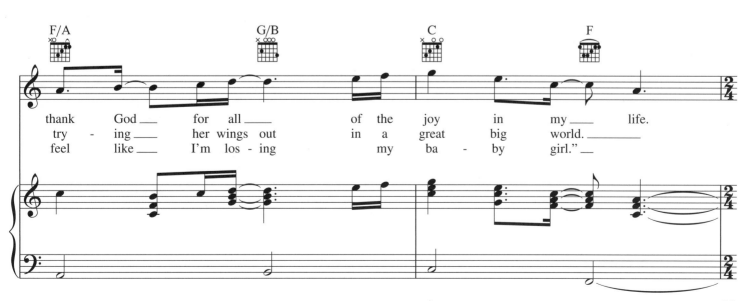

thank God ___ for all ___ of the joy in my ___ life.
try - ing ___ her wings out in a great big world. _____
feel like ___ I'm los - ing my ba - by girl." ___

I sure tried." —
cheek this time." —
dy, don't cry." —

Oh, with all that I've — done wrong, — I must have done some - thing right _____ to de - serve { a her { her

hug } love } ev -'ry morn - ing and but - ter - fly kiss - es — at night. —
love }

25

this is what _ love _ is. _ I know I've got-ta let _ her go, but I'll

al - ways _ re-mem-ber _ ev-'ry hug in the morn - ing and

molto rit.   *a tempo*

but - ter-fly kiss - es. _

molto rit.

Celebration

Words and Music by
Ronald Bell, Claydes Smith,
George Brown, James Taylor,
Robert Mickens, Earl Toon,
Dennis Thomas, Robert Bell
and Eumir Deodato

bra - tion. ___ We gon' cel - e - brate ___ and have a good ___ time. _____

It's time to come to - geth - er; it's up to you; ___

what's your pleas - ure? _____ Ev - 'ry - one a - round the world, come on!

(1., 2.) *Instrumental*
(3., 4.) Cel - e - brate good times, come on!

31

Fever

Words and Music by
John Davenport and Eddie Cooley

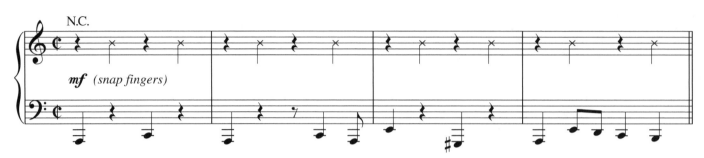

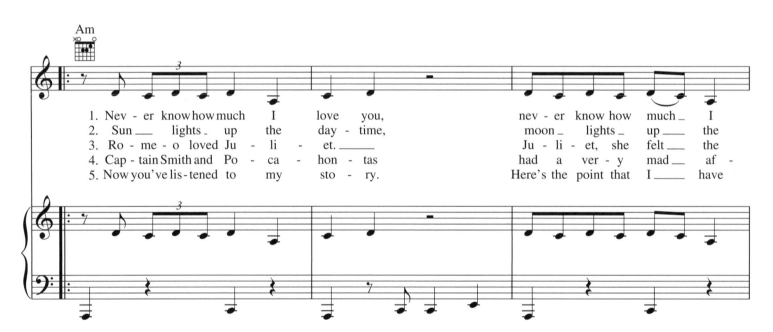

1. Nev - er know how much I love you,   nev - er know how much __ I
2. Sun __ lights __ up the day - time,   moon __ lights __ up __ the
3. Ro - me - o loved Ju - li - et. ___   Ju - li - et, she felt __ the
4. Cap - tain Smith and Po - ca - hon - tas   had a ver - y mad __ af -
5. Now you've lis - tened to my sto - ry.   Here's the point that I ___ have

care.   When you put your arms a - round me,   I get a
night.   I ___ light __ up when you call my name,   and you
same.   When he put his arms a - round her,   he said,
fair.   When her dad - dy tried to kill him,   she said,
made.   Chicks were born to give you fe - ver,   be it

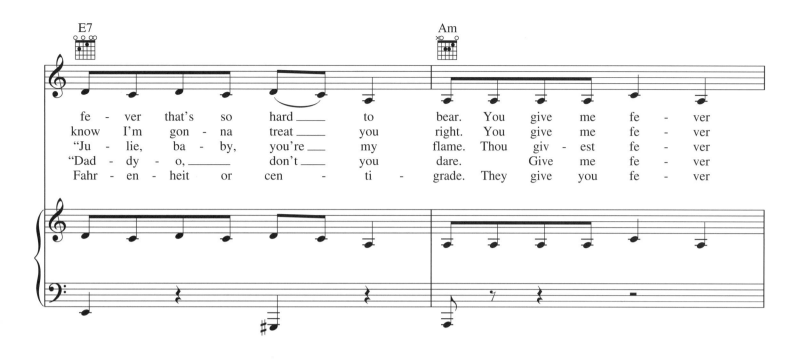

fe - ver that's so hard ___ to bear. You give me fe - ver
know I'm gon - na treat ___ you right. You give me fe - ver
"Ju - lie, ba - by, you're ___ my flame. Thou giv - est fe - ver
"Dad - dy - o, ___ don't ___ you dare. Give me fe - ver
Fahr - en - heit or cen - ti - grade. They give you fe - ver

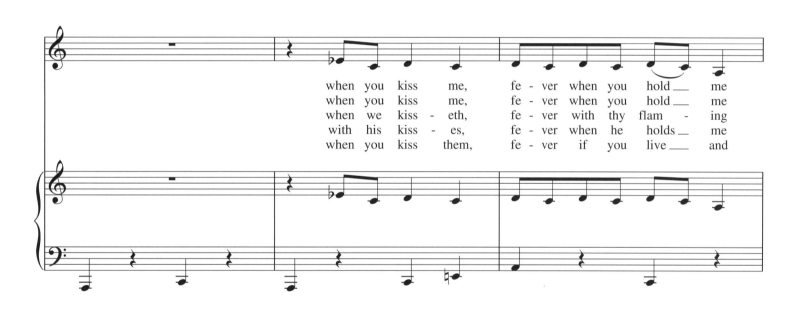

when you kiss me, fe - ver when you hold ___ me
when you kiss me, fe - ver when you hold ___ me
when we kiss - eth, fe - ver with thy flam - ing
with his kiss - es, fe - ver when he holds ___ me
when you kiss them, fe - ver if you live ___ and

tight, fe - ver in the morn - ing,
tight, fe - ver in the morn - ing,
youth. Fe - ver, I'm a - fire. ___
tight. Fe - ver, I'm his mis - sus. Oh,
learn. Fe - ver till you siz - zle,

fe - ver all through the night.
fe - ver all through the
Fe - ver, yeah, I burn for - sooth."
Dad - dy, won't you treat him right?"
what a love - ly way to

night. Ev - 'ry - bod - y's got the fe - ver; that is some - thing

you all know. Fe - ver is - n't such a new thing;

fe - ver start - ed long a - go. burn.

Father and Daughter

Words and Music by
Paul Simon

and nev-er leave 'til I leave you with a sweet dream _____ in your

head.

I'm gon-na watch you

shine, gon-na watch you grow. _____ Gon-na paint a

sign so you'll al-ways know, _____ as long as _____

40

Instrumental solo

D.S. al Coda II

CODA II

you.

Friends

Words and Music by
Michael W. Smith and Deborah D. Smith

Packing up ___ the dreams ___ God plant - ed
With the faith ___ and love ___ God's giv - en

in the fer - tile soil ___ of ___ you, _____
spring - ing from ___ the hope ___ we ___ know, _____

keep the love _ that keeps _ us strong. And _

friends are friends _ for - ev - er if the Lord's the Lord _ of them, _ and a

friend will not _ say "nev - er" 'cause the wel - come will _ not end. _ Though it's

hard to let _ you go, _ in the Fa - ther's hands _ we know _ that a

life - time's not ___ too long ___ to live ___ as friends. ___

And ___ friends are friends ___ for - ev - er if the

Lord's the Lord ___ of them, ___ and a friend will not ___ say "nev - er" 'cause the

From This Moment On

Words and Music by
Shania Twain and R.J. Lange

(Spoken:) for better, for worse, I will love you with ev - 'ry beat __ of my heart. __

From this

Slowly

mo - ment life has be - gun. __ *Male:* From this mo - ment _____

you are the one. __ *Female:* Right be - side __ you *Both:* is where I be - long, _____

*Male vocals sung an octave higher throughout.

49

prom - ise you this. _____ There is noth - ing I would-n't give, _____

from this mo - ment on. ____

Female: You're the rea - son I ___ be - lieve _ in

love, _____

Male: and you're the an - swer to ___ my prayers _ from

Good Riddance
(Time of Your Life)

Words by
Billie Joe Armstrong

Music by Billie Joe Armstrong,
Frank E. Wright, III and Michael Pritchard

G5

Time grabs you by ___ the ___ wrist, di - rects ___ you where _ to ___
Hang it on ___ a ___ shelf _ in good ___ health and ___ good _

C2

D5

go.
time.

Em

So make the best ___ of ___ this test _
Tat - toos of mem - o - ries and dead _

D

C9

___ and don't ___ ask why. _____
___ skin ___ on trial. _____

G

Em

It's not a ques -
For what it's worth, _

D

- tion, but a les - son ___ learned _ in ___ time. }
___ it ___ was worth ___ all ___ the ___ while. }

C9

End solo }

G

It's

56

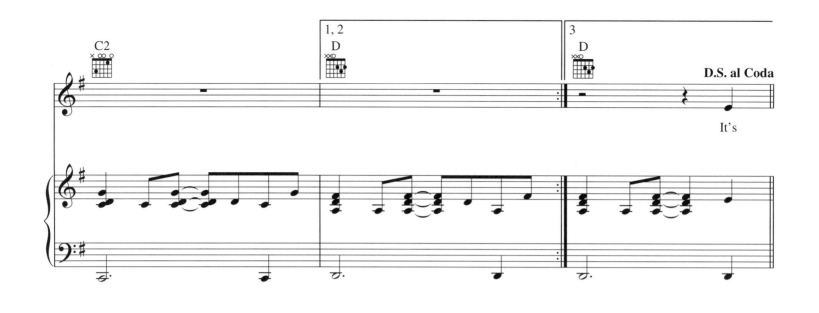

It's

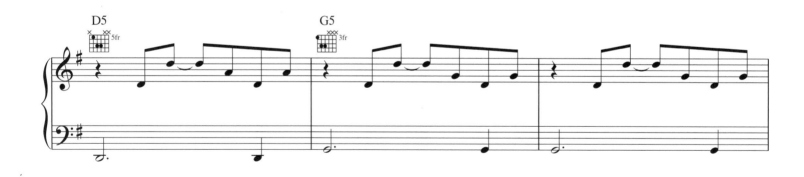

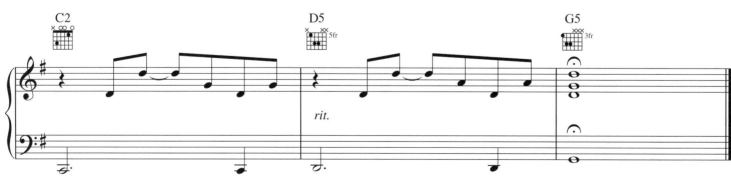

The Greatest Love of All

Words by
Linda Creed

Music by
Michael Masser

60

Have I Told You Lately

Words and Music by
Van Morrison

Have I told ___ you late - ly that I love you?

Have I told you there's no one else ___ a - bove ___ you?

Fill my heart ___ with glad - ness,

take a - way all ___ my sad - ness,

ease my trou-bles, that's __ what you do.

For the
Instrumental solo

morn - in' sun in all __ its glo - ry

greets the

day with hope and com - fort, too. __

You fill my life with laugh - ter

and some-how you make it bet - ter,

ease my trou - bles, that's ___ what you do. *Solo ends*

There's a love that's di - vine and it's yours and it's mine ___

___ like the sun. And at the end of the day

we should give thanks and pray ___ to the one, ___ to the one. ___ Have I

How Sweet It Is
(To Be Loved by You)

Words and Music by
Edward Holland, Lamont Dozier
and Brian Holland

You were bet-ter to me than I was to my-self, __ for me there's __ you and there ain't no-bod-y else. __ I want to stop and thank you, ba - by; I want __ to stop and thank you, ba - by, yes, I do. How sweet it is __ __ to be loved by you.

Repeat and Fade

Optional Ending

70

Hungry Eyes

from the Vestron Motion Picture DIRTY DANCING

Words and Music by
Franke Previte and John DeNicola

I Don't Want to Miss a Thing

from the Touchstone Picture ARMAGEDDON

Words and Music by
Diane Warren

ren - der.　　　I could stay lost in this mo - ment for -

ev - er.　　　Ev -'ry mo-ment spent with you___ is a mo ment I

treas - ure.　　　Don't wan - na close___ my eyes, ___

don't wan-na fall___ a - sleep, ___ 'coz I'd　miss you, ba - by, and I don't wan-na miss a　thing.___

'Coz e-ven when I dream of you, _ the sweet-est dream would nev-er do. _ I'd still

miss you ba-by, and I don't wan-na miss a thing. _

Lay-ing close to you, _ feel-ing your _ heart

beat-ing, and I'm won-d'ring what you're dream-ing, won-d'ring

be with you,__ right here __ with you, __ just like this. I just wan-na

hold __ you close, _____ feel your heart so close to mine, _____ and just

stay here in __ this mo-ment for all the rest of time. _

Ba - by, ba - by. ____ Don't wan - na close _ my eyes, _

don't wan-na fall __ a - sleep, __ 'coz I'd miss you, ba - by, and I don't wan-na miss a thing. __

__ 'Coz e - ven when I dream of you, __ the sweet-est dream would nev - er do. __ I'd still

miss you, ba - by, and I don't wan-na miss a thing. ___ Don't wan - na close __ my eyes, __

don't wan-na fall __ a - sleep, __ 'coz I'd miss you, ba - by, and I don't wan-na miss a thing. __

'Coz e - ven when I dream of you, _ the sweet-est dream would nev - er do. _ I'd still

miss you, ba - by, and I don't wan - na miss a thing. _____

Repeat ad lib. and Fade

I Gotta Feeling

Words and Music by
Will Adams, Allan Pineda,
Jaime Gomez, Stacy Ferguson,
David Guetta and Frederic Riesterer

I got-ta feel-

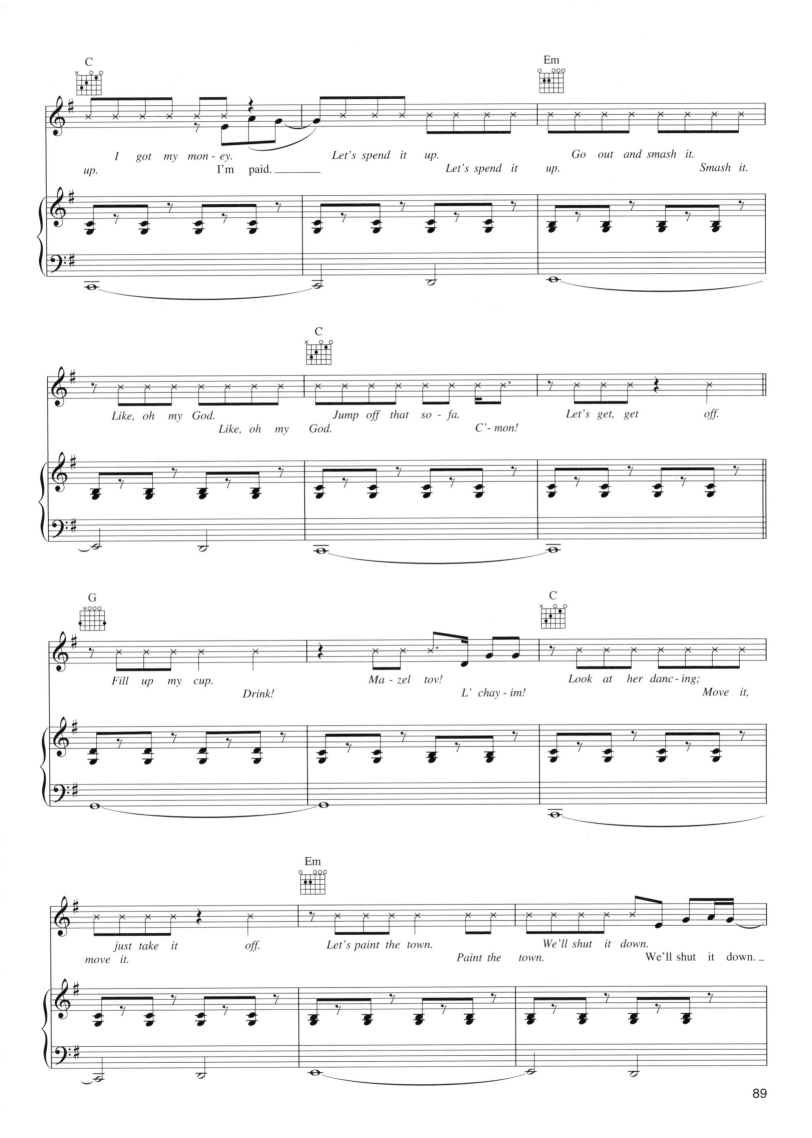

89

Let's burn the roof, and then we'll do it a-gain. _____ Let's do it, let's
Woo. _____

do it, let's do it, let's do it, _____ and do it, and do it. Let's live it up, and

do it, and do it, and do it, do it, do it. Let's do it. Let's do it. Let's

do it, do it, do it, do it. *Here we come, here we go. We got - ta rock.*

Eas - y come, eas - y go. Now we on top. Feel the shot, bod - y rock.

Rock it, don't stop. Round and round, up and down, a - round the clock.

Mon - day, Tues - day, Wednes - day and Thurs - day. Fri - day, Sat - ur - day.
Do it!

Sat - ur - day to Sun - day. Get, get, get, get, get with us. You know what we say, say:
Do it!

91

I Swear

Words and Music by
Frank Myers and Gary Baker

I see the ques - tions in ___ your eyes; ___ I know what's weigh -
I'll give you ev - 'ry - thing ___ I can; ___ I'll build your dreams

94

For bet- ter or worse, _ till death do us part, _____ I'll

love you with ev- er- y beat _____ of my heart, ___ I swear. _

_____ of my heart, _ I swear. _ *Instrumental solo*

96

97

I Will Always Love You

featured in THE BODYGUARD

Words and Music by
Dolly Parton

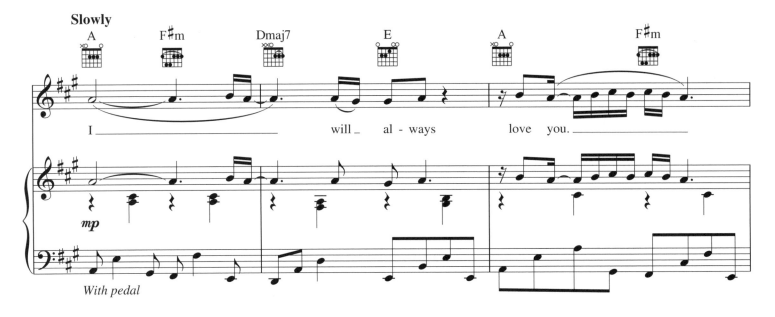

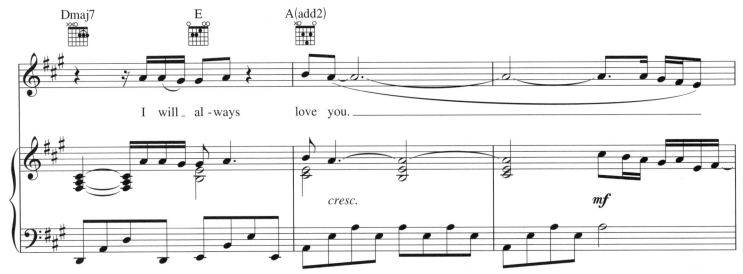

99

will _ al - ways _ love _ you. _____ I will al - ways _____ love _

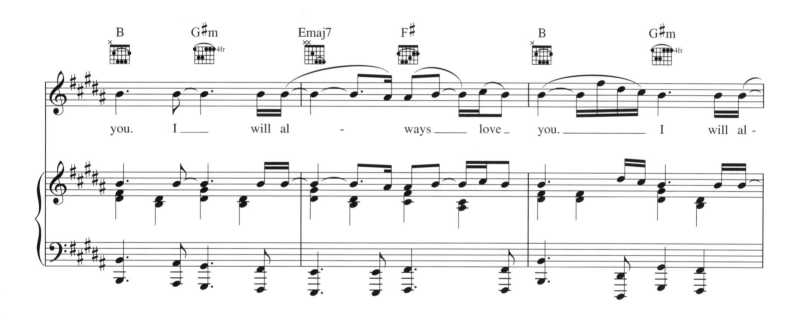

you. I _____ will al - ways _____ love _ you. _____ I will al -

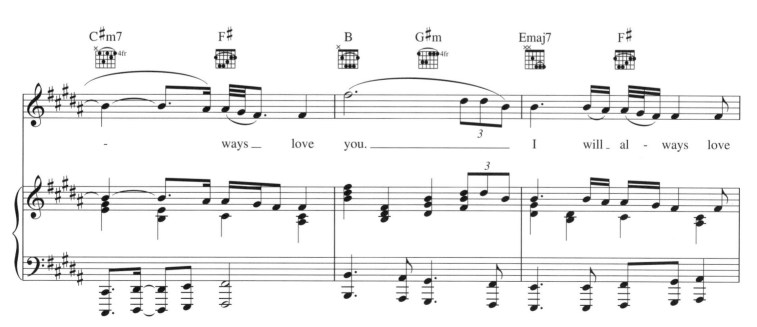

- ways _ love you. _____ I will _ al - ways love

Additional Lyrics

3. I hope life treats you kind.
   And I hope you have all you've dreamed of.
   And I wish to you, joy and happiness.
   But above all this, I wish you love.

I Won't Give Up

Words and Music by
Jason Mraz and Michael Natter

*Guitarists: Tune 6th string down to D.

No,___ I___ won't give up.___   I don't
wan-na be some-one who walks a-way so eas-i-ly. I'm here to stay and make the dif-fer-ence that
I can make.___   Our
dif-f'renc-es, they do a lot to teach us how to   use the tools and gifts we got; yeah, we got a lot___

at stake. And in the end, you're still my friend; at least we did in-tend for us to work. We did-n't break; we did-n't burn. We had to learn how to bend with-out the world cav-ing in. I had to learn what I got and what I'm not and who I

I'll Be There for You

(Theme from "Friends")

Words by
David Crane, Marta Kauffman,
Allee Willis, Phil Solem
and Danny Wilde

Music by
Michael Skloff

111

love life's D. O. A. _____   (1., 3.) It's like _____ you're al -
things are go - ing great. _____   (2.) Your moth - er warned _

- ways stuck _____ in sec - ond gear. _____   Well, it
_____ you there'd _ be days like these. _____   But she

has - n't been _ your day, _____ your week, _ your month, _ or e - ven your
did - n't tell _ you when _ the world _ has brought you down to your

year.   But _____ year. _____
knees,   that

112

No one could ev - er know_ me, no one could ev -

- er see_ me. Seems you're the on - ly one_ who knows_

what it's like to be___ me. Some - one to face___

the day___ with, make it through all____ the rest___ with,

some - one I'll al - ways laugh___ with. E - ven at my worst,___

___ I'm best___ with you. _____ Yeah!
(Inst. solo ad lib.)

Play cue notes 2nd time

I'll ___ be there for ___ you ___

I'll _____ be there for _____ you. _____

_____ I'll _____ be

there for _____ you _____ 'cause you're there for _____ me,

too. _____

(I've Had)
The Time of My Life
from DIRTY DANCING

Words and Music by
Franke Previte, John DeNicola
and Donald Markowitz

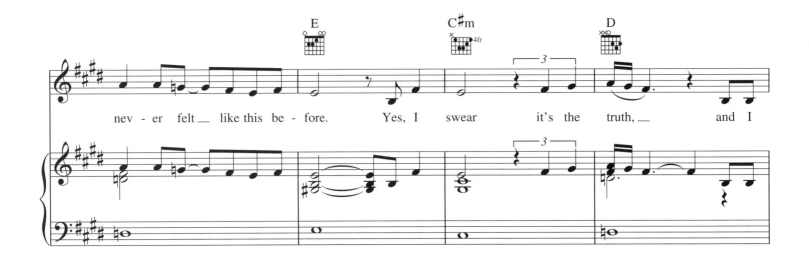

owe it all to you. _____

Male: I've been wait-ing for so long; _____ now I've

fi - n'lly found some-one ___ to stand by me.   *Female:* We saw the

writ - ing on the wall _____ as we felt this mag - i - cal ___ fan - ta -

sy. _____

Both: Now   with

pas - sion in our eyes _____ there's no   way we could _ dis - guise _____ it se - cret-

ly. _____

So   we

take each oth - er's hand _____ 'cause we   seem to un - der - stand _ the ur - gen-

just let it go; ___ don't be a-fraid to lose con-trol. ___

Female: Yes, I know what's on ___ your mind when you say ___ stay with me to-

night. ___ *Male:* Stay ___ with me. Just re-mem-ber, you're the

one thing ___ *Female:* I ___ can't get e-nough of. *Male:* So I'll tell you

In My Daughter's Eyes

Words and Music by
James Slater

strong and wise, ___ and I know ___ no fear. But the truth ___ is
turns to light ___ and the world ___ is at peace. This mir - a - cle ___ God

plain to see, ___ she was sent ___ to res - cue me. ___ I see who ___ I ___
gave to me ___ gives me strength ___ when I am weak. ___ I find rea - son ___

___ wan - na be ___ in my daugh - ter's ___ eyes.
___ to be - lieve ___ in my daugh - ter's ___

In my daugh - ter's ___ eyes. And when she wraps her

hand a-round my fin-ger al-ways puts a smile __ in __ my heart. __ Ev-'ry-thing be-

comes a lit-tle clear-er. I re-al-ize what life __ is all a-bout. It's hang-ing on when your

heart has had __ e-nough. It's giv-ing more when you feel __ like giv-ing up. _____ I've

seen the light. __ It's in my daugh - ter's eyes.

some - day leave, _ may - be raise ___ a fam - i - ly, when I'm gone ___ I

hope you'll see how hap - py she made ___ me, for I'll be

there in my daugh - ter's eyes.

In My Life

Words and Music by
John Lennon and Paul McCartney

134

Isn't She Lovely

Words and Music by
Stevie Wonder

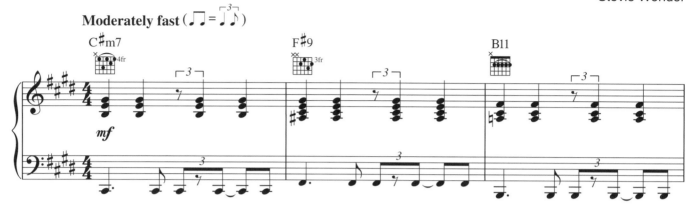

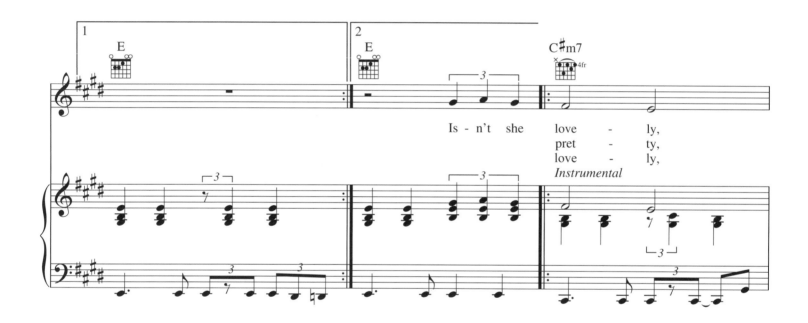

Is - n't she love - ly,
pret - ty,
love - ly,

Instrumental

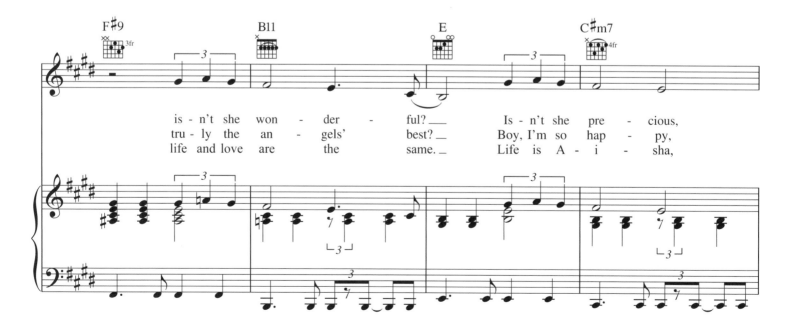

is - n't she won - der - ful? __ Is - n't she pre - cious,
tru - ly the an - gels' best? __ Boy, I'm so hap - py,
life and love are the same. __ Life is A - i - sha,

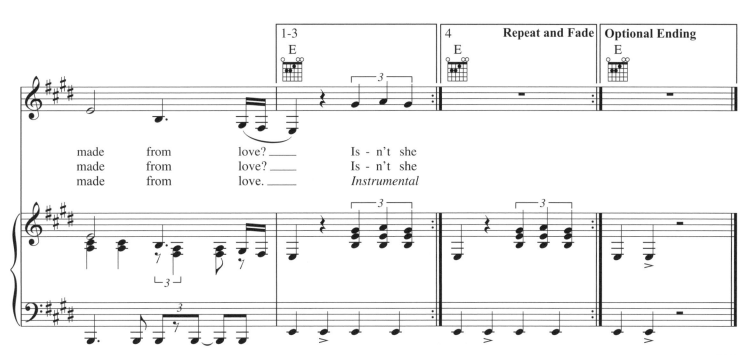

less than one min - ute old? ____ I nev - er thought ____ through love we'd be ____
we have been heav - en blessed. _ I can't be - lieve ____ what God has done, ____
the mean-ing of her name. ____ Lon - die, it could ____ have not been done ____

_____ mak - ing one as love - ly ____ as she. ____ But is - n't she love - ly,
_____ through us He's giv - en life ____ to one. ____ But is - n't she love - ly,
_____ with - out you who con - ceived ____ the one. ____ That's so ver - y love - ly,

made from love? ____ Is - n't she
made from love? ____ Is - n't she
made from love. ____ *Instrumental*

1-3 E   **4** E   **Repeat and Fade**   **Optional Ending** E

137

Last Dance

Words and Music by
Paul Jabara

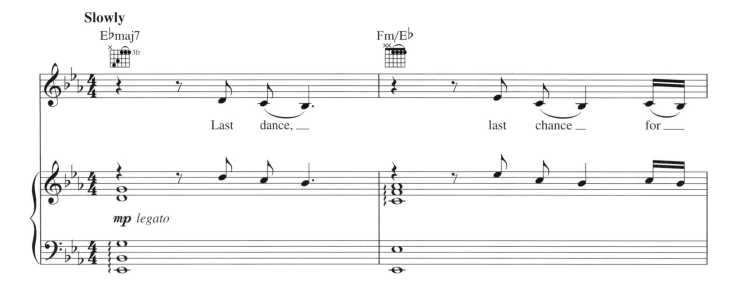

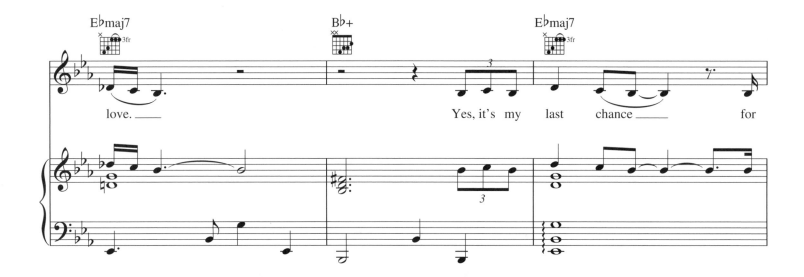

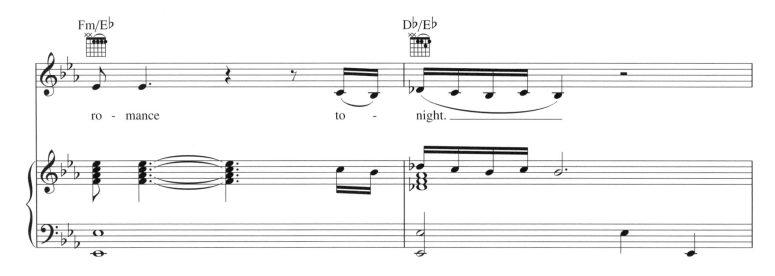

I need you by me, be-

side me _____ to guide me; to hold me; to

scold me, 'cause when I'm bad, I'm so, so bad. _____

Medium Disco beat

So let's dance _____ the last dance, _____

139

140

night. _____ Oh, _____ I need you by _

me, be - side me _____ to guide _

me; to hold _ me, to scold _ me, 'cause when I'm bad, _

I'm so, so bad. _____ So let's dance the

Lean on Me

Words and Music by
Bill Withers

I'll help you car - ry on, _____

for ___ it won't be long _____ 'til I'm gon - na need __

__ some - bod - y to lean _____ on. ___

Please ___ swal - low your pride _____ if I have things __

150

Legs

Words and Music by
Billy F Gibbons, Dusty Hill
and Frank Lee Beard

legs. _____
hair _____
legs. _____

She knows how to use ___ them. _

down to her fan - ny. _

She knows how to use ___ them. _

(8vb)

C#5

She nev - er begs. _____
She's kind - a jet - set.
She nev - er begs. _____

She knows how to
Try un - do her
Knows how to

E5

choose _ them. _
pan - ties. _
choose _ them. _

She hold - in' leg, _____
Ev - 'ry time she's danc - in'
She got a dime _____

won - derin' how to feel ___ them. ___
she knows ___ what to do. _____
all of the time.

Would ___ you get be-
Ev - 'ry - bod - y
Stays ___ out at

C#5

hind _____ them _____
wants ___ to see, _____
night, _____

if you could on - ly find them? _____
see if she can use it. _____
mov - in' through ___ time. _____

A5

She's my ba - - by,
She's so ___ fine. _____
Whoa, I want _____ her.

she's my ba -
She's all ___
Shit, I got to

8vb

loco

right. _

Guitar solo ad lib.

C#5

E5

Repeat and Fade

Optional Ending

Let's Get It On

Words and Music by
Marvin Gaye and Ed Townsend

Slow Soul beat

I've _ been real-ly try - in', ba - by, try-in' to hold _ back this feel in' for so _ long. And if you feel like _ I feel, _ ba-by, then come on, _ on, _ come on. Ooh, _ let's get it on. Ow, _

Love and Marriage

Words by
Sammy Cahn

Music by
James Van Heusen

165

Love and mar - riage, love and mar - riage, go to - geth - er like a

horse and car - riage. Dad was told by Moth - er, you can't have one, you

can't have none, you can't have one with - out the oth -

er.

er.

Mission: Impossible Theme

from the Paramount Motion Picture MISSION: IMPOSSIBLE

By Lalo Schifrin

Moderately, with drive

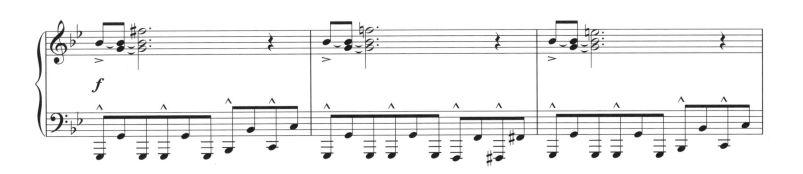

My Girl

Words and Music by
William "Smokey" Robinson and Ronald White

sweet-er song _____ than the birds in the trees.

D.S. al Coda

Well, _

CODA

(My girl.) Ooh, _____ hoo. _____

(Hey, hey, hey.)

(Hey, hey, hey.)

172

(Talk - in' 'bout my girl, my girl,

e - ven got the month of May with my girl.

my girl, whoa, whoa.)

Talk - in' 'bout, talk - in' 'bout, talk - in' 'bout my girl.

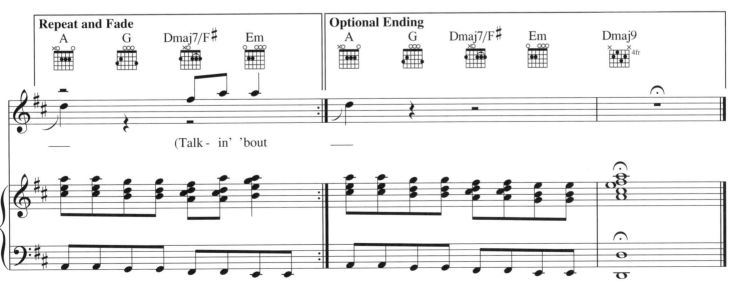

Repeat and Fade

(Talk - in' 'bout

Optional Ending

Not While I'm Around

from SWEENEY TODD

Words and Music by
Stephen Sondheim

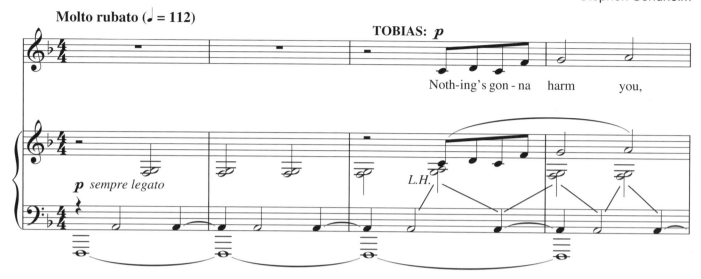

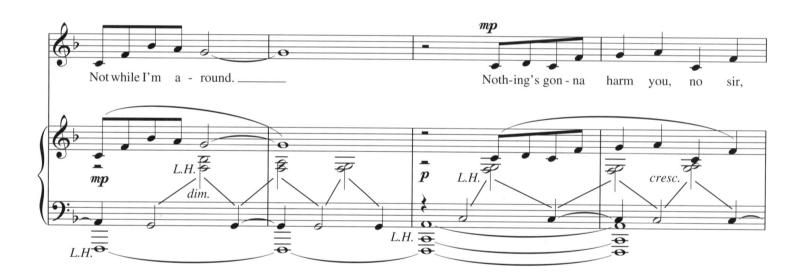

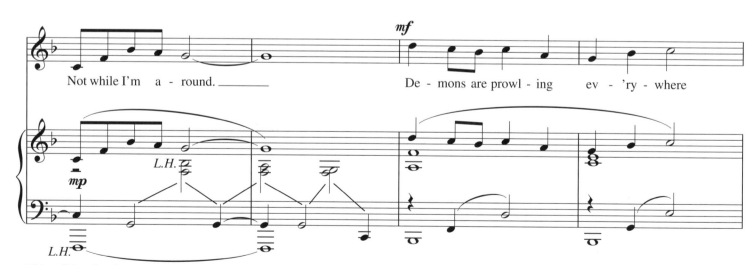

This edition has been transposed down a minor third from the original key of A-flat Major.

now - a - days. _____ I'll send 'em howl - ing, I don't care...

I got ways. _____

No one's gon - na hurt you, No one's gon - na dare. _____

Oth - ers can de - sert you, Not to wor - ry, Whis - tle, I'll be there. _____

De - mons 'll charm you with a smile For a while, But in time

Noth-ing can harm you, Not while I'm a - round. _____

Più mosso, sempre rubato

Not to wor - ry, Not to wor - ry, I may not be

smart but I ain't dumb. I can do it, Put me to it,

178

poco rit.

Show me some-thing I can o - ver - come. Not to wor - ry,

a tempo

mum. Be - ing close and be - ing clev - er ain't like be - ing

true. I don't need to, I won't nev - er hide a thing from

rit. **mp** **Tempo primo** **mp**

you, Like some. No one's gon - na

rit. e dim. *mp espressivo* *mp*

hurt you, No one's gon-na dare. _____ Oth-ers can de-

sert you, Not to wor-ry, Whis tle, I'll be there. _____ De-mons 'll charm you

with a smile For a while, But in time Noth-ing's gon-na harm you,

Not while I'm a - round. _____

180

On a Night Like This

Words and Music by
Dave Barnes

love hangs _ thick _ like these _ wil - low _____ leaves. _____ I've

hid my - self _____ a - way from this, _____ but your

sil - hou - ette is _____ the Ju - das kiss. _____

On a Ju - das kiss. _____

Save the Best for Last

Words and Music by
Wendy Waldman, Phil Galdston
and Jon Lind

185

To Coda ⊕

186

Just when I thought _____ our chance ___ had passed, _

you go and save _____ the best ___ for last. ___

All of the nights ___ ___

one thing   you   can't   see.   Some-times   the   snow _

You went and saved ___ the best ___ for last. _____

Yeah. _____

Shower the People

Words and Music by
James Taylor

One thing can lead __ to an - oth - er; _____ it does - n't
Once you tell some - bod - y _____ the way that you feel, you can

take an - y sac - ri - fice. __ Oh, _____ fa - ther and moth - er, sis -
feel it be - gin - ning to ease. __ I think it's true what they say a - bout the

ter and broth - er, if it feels nice __ don't __ think twice. __ Just
squeak - y wheel, _____ al - ways get - ting the grease. __ Bet - ter __ to

show - er the peo - ple you love __ with love; _ show them the way _ that you feel. __

1., 2., etc. Show-er the peo - ple you love ___ with love. ___
3., etc. *(See additional lyrics for vocal ad lib.)*

Repeat and Fade

Show them the way ___ that you feel. ___

Additional Lyrics

They say in every life,
They say the rain must fall.
Just like a pouring rain,
Make it rain.
Love is sunshine.

A Song for Mama

from the Fox 2000 Motion Picture SOUL FOOD

Words and Music by
Babyface

195

and it just would-n't feel right
You al-ways did un-der-stand.

if I did-n't have you by my side.
You gave me strength to go on.

There

You were there for me to love and care for me when
was so man-y times look-ing back when I was

skies were grey.
so a-fraid,

When-ev-er I was down, you were al-ways there to
and then you'd come to me and say to me I could

com-fort me.
face an-y-thing.

And no one else can be what you have been to me. You will
And no one else can do what you have done for me. You'll

Still the One

Words and Music by
John Hall and Johanna Hall

Rock Boogie beat

We're still hav - ing fun, _____ and you're still _____ the one. ___

You're ___   You ___ are ___

Yeah, _____ and you're still

204

The Stripper

Music by David Rose

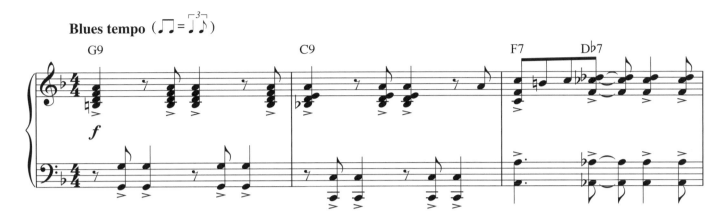

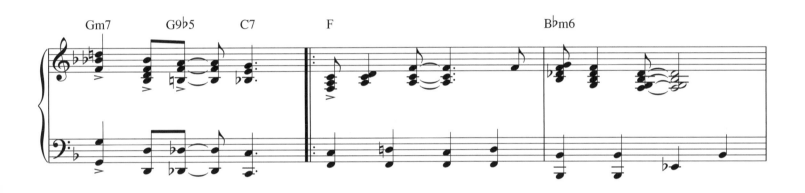

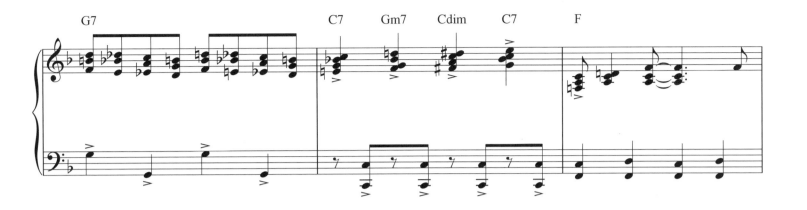

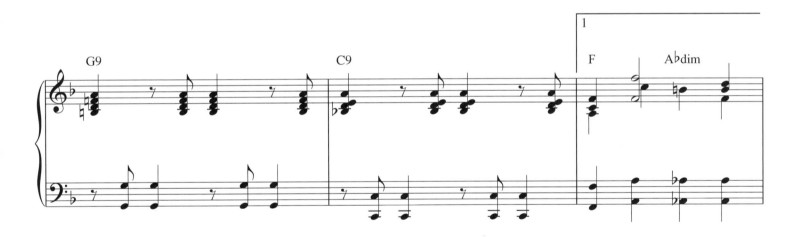

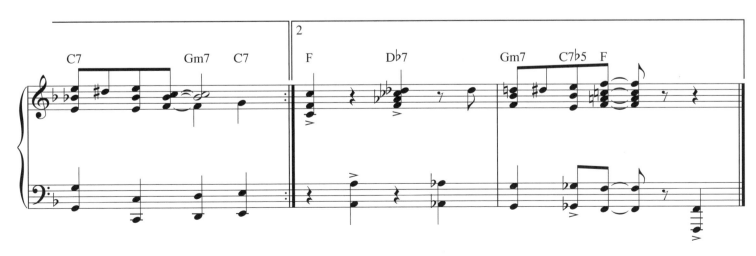

Sunrise, Sunset

from the Musical FIDDLER ON THE ROOF

Words by
Sheldon Harnick

Music by
Jerry Bock

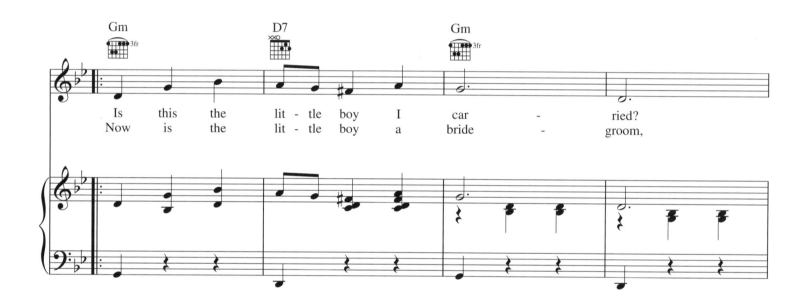

Is this the lit-tle boy I car - ried?
Now is the lit-tle boy a bride - groom,

Is this the lit-tle girl at play? I don't re -
now is the lit-tle girl a bride? Un - der the

small? _____

pass. _____

Sun - rise, _____ sun - set, sun - rise, _____ sun - set, swift - ly _____

_____ flow the days. _____ Seed - lings turn

o - ver-night to sun - flow'rs, blos - som - ing e - ven as we

That's What Friends Are For

Words by
Carole Bayer Sager

Music by
Burt Bacharach

That's what friends are for.

{ For good ___ times, and bad ___ times }
{ In good ___ times, in bad ___ times }

I'll be on ___ your side for-ev - er - more.

That's what friends ___ are

To Coda

1

for

2

for.

D.S. al Coda

CODA

for.

Repeat and Fade

Vocal ad lib.

They Can't Take That Away from Me

from SHALL WE DANCE

Music and Lyrics by
George Gerswhin and Ira Gershwin

Our ro - mance won't end on a sor - row - ful note, though by to - mor - row you're gone; _____ the song is end - ed, but as the song-writ - er wrote, the

can't take that a-way from me! The way your smile just beams, ___ the way you sing off key, ___

the way you haunt my dreams, _____ no, no, they

can't take that a-way from me! ___ We may nev - er, nev - er meet a - gain on the

bump-y road to love, still I'll al - ways, al - ways keep the mem - 'ry

Through the Years

Words and Music by
Steve Dorff and Marty Panzer

made.
way.

And I'm _____ so glad I've stayed _____
As long _____ as it's o - kay,

_____ right here with you _____
_____ I'll stay with you _____

through the
through the

years.

I

years.

doubt, we'd al - ways work ___ things ___ out. I've
day, you've kissed ___ my tears ___ a - way. As

learned what love's a - bout ___ by lov - ing
long as it's o - kay, ___ I'll stay with

you ___ through the years.
you ___ through the the

Through ___ the years. ___

Truly

Words and Music by
Lionel Richie

heels   with your   love. _____   I   need _____ you, _____

and   with your   love _____   I'm   free. _____   And

tru - ly, _____   you know you're   all   right ___

with _____   me. _____

Unforgettable

Words and Music by
Irving Gordon

229

C/E   Gm6/E   A7   D9

how the thought of you does things_ to me. Nev - er be - fore ____

Db   D7

has some - one been more ____

G   Gdim

un - for - get - ta - ble, ____ in ev - 'ry way, _____

C

and for - ev - er - more, ___ that's how you'll

The Way You Look Tonight

from SWING TIME

Words by
Dorothy Fields

Music by
Jerome Kern

Lyrics:

Some - day, when I'm aw - f'ly low, when the world is
love - ly, with your smile so warm, and your cheek so

cold, I will feel a glow just think - ing of you
soft, there is noth - ing for me but to love you,

and the way you look to - night.
just the way you look to - night.

Oh, but you're

never, nev - er change, keep that breath - less charm,

won't you please ar - range it, 'cause I love you,

rall.

just the way you look to - night.

a tempo

Just the way you look to - night. _____

rall.

We Are Family

Words and Music by
Nile Rodgers and Bernard Edwards

Liv - ing life is fun, and we've just be - gun to get our share ___ of this world's

de - lights. ___ High hopes we have ___ for the fu -

- ture, and our goal's in sight. No, we don't get de - pressed. ___

___ Here's what we call ___ our ___ Gold - en Rule:

We've Only Just Begun

Words and Music by
Roger Nichols and Paul Williams

sun _____ we fly. _____ So man-y roads to choose,
comes _____ we smile, _____ so much of life a-head,

To Coda ⊕

we start out walk-ing and learn to run. _____ And yes,we've just be-
we'll find a place _ where there's room to grow. _____

gun. _____ Shar-ing hor-i-zons that are

new to us, watch-ing the signs a-long the way.

242

What a Wonderful World

Words and Music by
George David Weiss and Bob Thiele

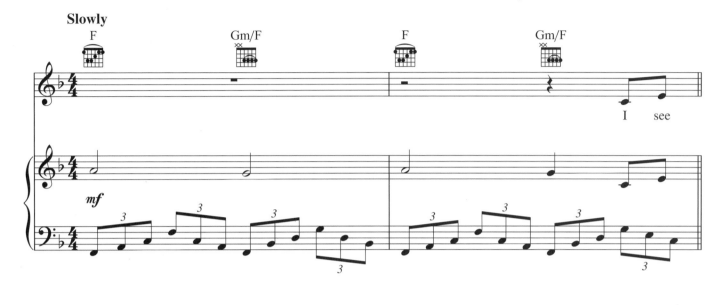

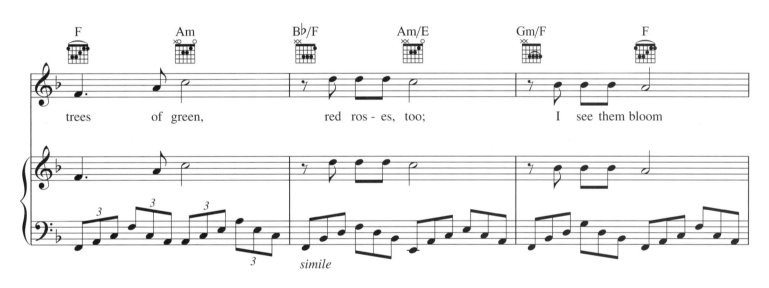

ba - bies cry, I watch them grow; they'll learn much more than

I'll ___ ev-er know, ___ and I think ___ to my-self, "What a won - der - ful

world." _____ Yes, I think to my - self,

"What a won-der-ful world." _____

Rubato

simile

rit.

246

The Wind Beneath My Wings

from the Original Motion Picture BEACHES

Words and Music by
Larry Henley and Jeff Silbar

'cause you are the wind___ be-neath my wings.

It might have ap-peared___ to go un-

no - ticed   that I've got it all___   here in my

heart.   I want you to know___ I know the

Wonderful Tonight

Words and Music by
Eric Clapton

is that you just don't re - al - ize___ how much___ I love___ you.

D.S. al Coda

CODA

Oh, my dar - ling, you are won - der - ful___ to - night."___

rit.

254

Y.M.C.A.

Words and Music by
Jacques Morali, Henri Belolo
and Victor Willis

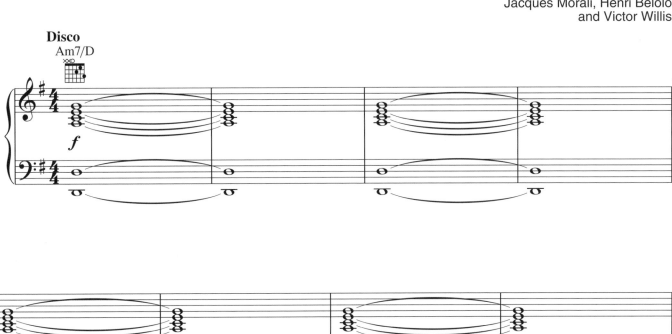

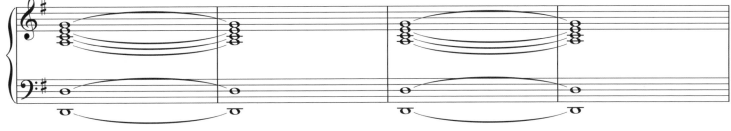

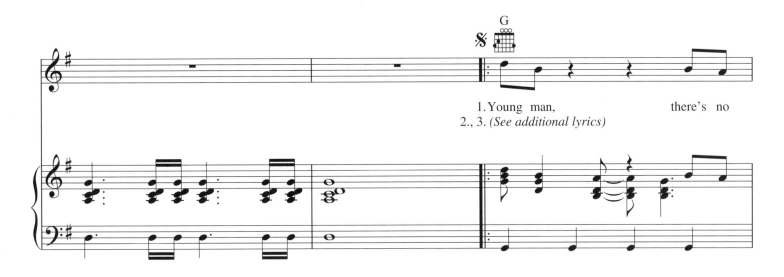

1. Young man,   there's no
2., 3. *(See additional lyrics)*

need to feel down. ___ I said, young man, pick your-

self off the ground. ___ I said, young man, 'cause you're

in a new town ___ there's no need to ___ be ___ un-hap-py.

Young man, there's a place you can go, ___ I said,

256

young man, when you're short on your dough. You can stay there and I'm

sure you will find ___ man-y ways to ___ have ___ a good time.

Chorus

N.C.

It's fun to stay at the Y. M. C. A.

It's fun to stay at the ___ Y. M. C. A. ___

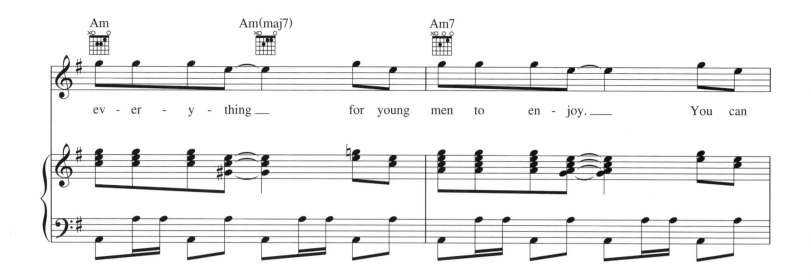

ev-er-y-thing ___ for young men to en-joy. ___ You can

Repeat ad lib. and Fade

hang out with all ___ the boys. ___ It's fun to stay at the

Additional Lyrics

2. Young man, are you listening to me?
   I said, young man, what do you want to be?
   I said, young man, you can make real your dreams
   But you've got to know this one thing.

   No man does it all by himself.
   I said, young man, put your pride on the shelf.
   And just go there to the Y.M.C.A.
   I'm sure they can help you today.
   Chorus

3. Young man, I was once in your shoes.
   I said, I was down and out and with the blues.
   I felt no man cared if I were alive.
   I felt the whole world was so jive.

   That's when someone come up to me
   And said, "Young man, take a walk up the street.
   It's a place there called the Y.M.C.A.
   They can start you back on your way."
   Chorus

260

You Are the Sunshine of My Life

Words and Music by
Stevie Wonder

263

You Sexy Thing

Words and Music by
E. Brown

How did you know   I   need-ed you so bad - ly?
Did you know   you're   ev -'ry-thing I   prayed _ for?

How did you know   I'd   give my heart glad - ly?   Yes - ter - day _   I was
Did you know?   Ev -'ry night and   day for   ev -'ry   day, _   giv-in'

one of the lone - ly   peo - ple.   Now you're ly - ing   close to me,
love   and   sat - is - fac - tion.   Now you're ly - ing   next to me,

mak-in' love to   me. _   I be-lieve in mir-a cles.   Where you from, _
giv-in' it to   me. _

You're Still the One

Words and Music by
Shania Twain and R.J. Lange

You're still the one I kiss good-night.

night. ____ You're still ____ the one.

(You're still the one.) ____

night.

I'm so glad we made ____ it. Look how far ____ we've come, my ba-by. ____